ZC HORSES
LUKE
THE FIRST!

Diane W. Keaster

illustrated by Debbie Page

1

ISBN 0-9721496-3-5

Printed in Canada

ZC HORSES

LUKE

THE FIRST!

To my brother Gary for always being there to help me and for letting me ride his 'big horse' when I was little.

ZC HORSES
SERIES

Be part of them all!

Chick - The Beginning!

Chick - The Saddle Horse!

Chick - The Mom!

Luke - The First!

And Many More!

ZC HORSES
LUKE
THE FIRST!

INDEX

1

THE RANCH

There are many different places to grow up. Some kids grow up in the city. Some grow up in small towns in the desert. Some grow up in a town in the mountains. Some grow up living in a small house. Some grow up living in a great big house. I feel where I grew up was best.

It was on a beautiful working ranch. Our house was in a coulee. A coulee is a small valley. There were many large, billowing trees always gently waving to you with their many green hands.

Once on top of the coulee, we could see the gigantic mountain ranges. At times, they wore the fluffy clouds as a hat. They appeared blue at a distance.

The corral surrounded a portion of Box Elder Creek. A creek is a small stream. A person from Montana says 'creek' so it sounds like 'stick'. The corral was made of wooden poles that had become grey from the weather. A red barn sat in the middle of it all. Looking across at the corral, day dreaming, the colors of the red barn, grey poles, green trees, silver creek, and whatever color of horses or cows rested there, joined together.

Spring time was a beautiful time on the ranch. The wild flowers that dotted the hillsides were awakening. Blue, pink, yellow, red dots popped up as stars do at night. The trees allowed their soft leaves to come out. Babies of all sorts were to be seen everywhere. Kittens, puppies, bunnies, calves (baby cows), foals (baby horses), chicks and so many more new babies were livening up the country.

A person is always busy on the

ranch. There are many things to do. One job to be done in the Spring was branding the baby calves. A brand is a special combination of letters or pictures that are put on livestock so a rancher can see what animal he or she owns. Each rancher has their own brand that no one else has. The brand is placed on one side or the other of the horse or cow.

In the Spring, when the calves are a few weeks old, they need their owner's brand put on them. With the brand, they can always be placed back with their mom if they get separated.

Branding day was always exciting. First, all the cows and calves needed to be gathered. This was done riding horses. That was my favorite part!

When gathering the cows and calves, my brothers, father and I rode. A good friend named Roger also rode. He rode Peppy, a red roan, which means there are red and white hairs scattered through the coat. The horses sometimes used by my brothers were Baldy, Sarge, Eagle, Smokey, Buck and others.

All the riders spread out to get around all the cows and calves. Pete, my small dog that looked like a police dog, trotted along with us. Since the calves were young, we had to take our time.

The mother cows got very nervous if their babies were not right with them. They bellered out their "Moooos". The babies cried back.

At branding time, sometimes the cows and their babies were in a pasture called the 'Spring Pasture'. It was called that because there was a big spring in the pasture. That is where water comes bubbling up out of the ground.

This land was once owned by my great-grandfather. When he was fifteen years old, he snuck onto a ship in a distant land called Ireland. It is far across the Atlantic Ocean. When he got to America, he travelled to Montana and bought the ranch where we were branding. He always had many horses and cows on his ranch. His brand was a 'Z' with a 'C' connected to it. It was fun to imagine him placing his brand on his cows in that same pasture over 100 years earlier! His brand then became mine.

Once we got all of the cows and calves gathered into the corral, the calves had to be put into a different section. The cows continually called out to their babies. The calves continually cried back to their moms. The air was filled with noise! We had to holler to be heard above the commotion of the cows and calves.

Dust rolled through the corral as the cows nervously walked the

fence, trying to see their new-
borns. Calves kicked up even
more dust running back and forth.

Once the cows and calves were
split, we pushed the calves
through a long runway in the corral. Different ranchers brand dif-
ferently. Our calves lie on a table.
Once flat, we placed a branding
iron on them so that the brand
showed up on their side.

The irons were kept hot to sear the
hair of the calf into the form of the
brand. Smoke reached to the sky
from where the irons were heated.
This brand showed as the calf
grew.
When the calves got off the table,
they ran and bucked and kicked up

their heels, racing to their mothers as fast as they could. Pete trailed them to their moms.

The day was filled with a lot of action and excitement. Everyone had their job to do to make the branding day a success. If you were pushing the calves up to the table, your shins probably got kicked by the frisky calves. If you were grabbing the long iron with the brand, you got very tired.

No matter what job you had, it was rewarding to see the branded babies back with their moms so all would know who owned them. When the day was done, moms and children went back to playing, eating, and resting.

My wonderful horse, Chick, always loved gathering the cows for the branding.

Chick's favorite job, though, was rewarding for her!

2

CHICK THE MOM

Chick was a very special horse to me. She was a beautiful golden palomino. A palomino horse is yellow. Her mane and tail were as white as snow. Although we loved our many rides together, there came the time when I decided she should have a baby. A baby horse is called a foal. The job of being a mother was Chick's favorite. She was a fabulous mother to all her babies.

For Chick to become a mom, I had to find a father for the baby. This was an exciting time. I wanted to make sure I had the right stallion in mind to be the father of Chick's first baby. How special it would be!

In trying to decide what to do, I sat on a pole in the corral. It was one that crossed the creek rippling through. My brother's stallion, Printer, was in the corral. As I sat thinking, he wandered over to me. Putting his head up to me, I scratched his ears. That was it! Printer would be the father!

Printer was a beautiful, dark red stallion. His color was chestnut. He was a very friendly horse.

Chick's first baby would not be born for another eleven months. It was such a long wait! I was so excited!

During that eleven months, I pondered what color the baby would be. Would it be palomino, like Chick, or chestnut, like its father, Printer. Would it be a colt, a boy, or a filly, a girl? I knew it would

be friendly and gentle since its mom and dad were.

Chick was born on April 25. It was around that date that her first baby was to drop, or be born. I pampered Chick during those eleven months. I pampered her even more as April 25 got closer. All through the day and night, I checked on her.

April 24 finally came. By Chick's appearance, I was sure she would foal, or deliver her baby that night. Several times I went out into the starry night to see if she was okay. The stars twinkled at me like everything was normal. When I went out to the corral, Chick came sleepily up to me and pressed her

soft nose against me to pet. Gently
stroking her head, I talked to her.
She seemed rather sad.

Pete always went with me and sat patiently. He tried to figure out what was going on.

The last time I went out was dawn. The sun began to creep over the horizon. The horizon is where the sky meets the hill of the coulee. Since nothing had happened, I went back to bed.

Sleeping soundly, my mother's calls startled me. I could tell by the concerned look she wore that something was wrong. Hesitantly she said, "Chick had her baby, but it won't get up."

Frantically I sprung from my bed. I could not get out to the corral fast enough. Pete raced behind me.

Frost was resting upon the grey poles of the corral. There was Chick. She stood looking down at her baby. She threw a troubled look at me then put her nose gently on the foal. Nudging the foal gently, Chick nickered, or gave a soft whinny.

A lump formed in my throat. I was holding back tears.

What could I do?

3

BABY IN TROUBLE

"How could this have happened?, I questioned.

The foal stayed flat, not making a sound. After a baby is born, it needs to drink from its mother immediately to survive. That first drink is special. It is called 'colostrum'.

I had waited so long. Now the baby would not get up. I saw that it was a beautiful palomino, like Chick. It was a colt, a boy. Right away I tagged him 'Luke'.

Luke wore the same blaze as his mom. A blaze is a wide strip of white down a horse's face. If a horse is 'bald', its strip is wider, covering most of the face. His back, or hind leg on the right side had a sock. That means white far up its leg. A 'stocking' is much higher.

Chick once more glanced at me then back at her skinny baby. When a foal is born, it looks like it is all legs! Chick let a nicker slip from her sad lips. Then, happily, a soft nicker came from Luke!

Chick's furry ears stood straight up. She nickered louder and nudged Luke with her nose. Luke's head came up off the cold, hard ground. This time a full whinny shot from his mouth! With one jump, he was up! A new-born foal's legs are not

very strong. Luke wobbled by his mom. Chick's face was aglow! Pete's was, too! I knew mine was. Luke was so beautiful! Chick eased closer to him. Right away he began to nurse, or drink from Chick.

What a relief! Pete snuck towards Chick to see what this was beside her. Luke turned and inspected him. They got along great after approval of each other.

Once Luke had finished his first meal, he tried to run and buck. His weak legs would not allow such activity. Within a few hours, though, his legs were strong. Then he ran circles around his mom. Luke was so happy to be up running and bucking and playing. Toward the sky his heels went. Up in the air his front legs went. He would not stop!

Luke's lively disposition worried me. Now was the time to put on his little blue halter. A halter goes

over a horses nose and behind its
ears. It is used to lead the horse or
to tie them. It is usually made out
of nylon, leather or rope.

Luke studied me with worried
eyes as I eased up to him. He did
not know what to think.

Luke's soft, fuzzy ears turned backwards as I slowly situated my left arm around his chest and my right arm around his rear. Watching him romp friskily around his mom, I figured he would jump. To my surprise, he stood perfectly still. As I gently slipped the tiny blue halter over his nose, Luke turned his ears forward. If a horse has its ears forward, it feels comfortable. If the ears are back, the horse is questioning what is happening. I fastened the halter with no fight from Luke at all.

Once the halter is on a foal, the foal must learn to lead. Quite often, the foal will resist and pull back. Luke did just the opposite.

He followed right along behind me. Pete followed right along behind him!

I knew from the moment I touched Luke, he would be great to work with. He had a great personality and calm disposition, or attitude. He was very handsome, too, with his golden-colored coat, pure white mane and tail, and white stocking and blaze!

That is why I was so shocked when Luke decided to change his looks!

4

A NEW LOOK

Luke was such a joy to be around and handle. He always came right up to me to be caught. Chick had taught him not to be afraid of people.

Pete and Luke had a special relationship. When Luke was close in the pasture, Pete went out to visit with him. If Pete ran, off running went Luke. If Luke ran, off running went Pete. Sometimes they even ran at each other. Other times, they chased each other.

Luke always was very curious about things. He was continually in some sort of trouble. He was a typical kid!

One pasture where Luke and his mom dwelled had nice, green, rolling hills. Cattle also resided in

this pasture. The hillsides were dotted with red, black, and white as the cows contentedly grazed on the lush grass. Their babies romped around them just as Luke romped around his mom.

It was in this pasture I had ridden Chick into a bog when we were chasing a bull.

Luke also had made friends with many of the other horses pastured there. There was a roan, which is a blue-colored horse with black and white hairs through its body. Also pastured there was a bay which has a dark red body with a black mane and tail.

When they all ran, it was as if a

wave of blue, red, yellow, white, and brown was rolling across the fields.

This pasture was also home to rattlesnakes. It always worried me that Luke would get bit by one. Especially since he was so curious!

If a horse had its head down eating, a wretched rattlesnake may sneak up and bite the horse's nose. The nose then swells up like a hot-air balloon. If the horse first hears the snake's warning rattles, they usually get scared and run. I was worried Luke would be too curious to run if he heard the distinctive rattle. The rattle sounds like little rocks shaking in a tin can.

One day I went to check on Luke and his mom. When I got to the pasture, all I saw against the hill-sides were red, black, and white spots, the cows and calves. Scattered throughout these graz-ing, or eating animals, were dots of yellow, pink, purple and orange. The wild flowers decorated the fields as if decorating a cake.

As I neared the horses, I became very concerned. Luke was no where to be found. There was an old shed with a corral around it. The horses were standing around it to find shelter from the sizzling sun. The horses were bunched together in a ball of red, yellow, blue and brown. I bent over to look at their legs. Luke was the only one there with a sock, or white on his leg. I saw no white legs. I saw four yellow legs, which were Chick's. The rest were brown or black or red.

Looking all around the shed, I still did not find Luke. This pasture was always very windy. I covered my face as a whirlwind of dust showered us.

The horses decided to follow me. As they split up, I was amazed at

what I saw. There, standing in the middle, was Luke. His legs were solid black up to his knees and hocks. (The joints half way up a horse's legs in the front are its knees. The joints half way up its hind, or back, legs are its hocks.)

Luke obviously had been playing in the bog. Black mud hid his yellow legs and sock. What a sight he was! He looked like a beautiful palomino with four black stockings!

Relief came upon me knowing Luke had not been bit by a rattlesnake or worse.

There was a time, though, when I did not feel that relief.

5

THE ACCIDENT

Luke grew up to be a very hand-some horse. He had a wonderful disposition. The time came when he was old enough to leave his mother's side, or be weaned. He then could be put out to pasture by himself or with horses other than his mom.

Once Luke was in a pasture across

the road from our house. He was with a few other horses. There was a small pond where they could drink the cool water. Thick brush surrounding the pond acted as a shelter from the scorching sun and howling wind. The green grass was tall and waved as the breezes blew.

Quite often, the horses ran their fastest and hardest. Sometimes when a young horse is playing like this, they do not always pay attention to what is around. Luke must not have been paying attention one day.

Being so close to the house, I visited Luke often. The day he was not paying attention, I went to see him. As I got close to the horses, I saw Luke standing away from the herd. His head was hanging. I was used to seeing him running as fast as the wind with his head high in the air. As he ran, his white mane and tail flowed. Seeing him with his head almost touching the ground was a very scary sight.

At first, I started walking slowly to Luke. My pace quickened when I saw what had happened. My heart and steps were pounding at the same rate. The rate increased with every move.

As I neared Luke, he did not raise his head. Pain spewed from his eyes as he tried to look at me.

The front part of Luke's beautiful golden body was bright red. He must have run into something while he was playing. A tremendous gash now covered his shoulder.

It was obvious Luke was in a great amount of agony. I knew he had to immediately get to a veterinarian, or animal doctor. With such a severe injury, I did not know how Luke could survive.

Once to his clinic, the veterinarian was extremely concerned about Luke. He lamented, "I have never seen such a bad wound. I will have to see if I can fix it."

Luke had to be given medication to make him drowsy. That way, he would not mind the vet, or veterinarian, working on him.

The vet stitched up Luke's muscle and skin like he was mending a shirt. Luke dozed throughout the whole procedure. There ended up being many stitches in his shoulder.

Once completed, the vet sighed, "That is all I can do. Hopefully he will be able to walk again."

WALK AGAIN!!! I could not believe my ears. How could this happen to such a beautiful, kind animal. I was too shocked to cry.

Time passed ever so slowly during Luke's mending. It was difficult for him to get around. Pain showed in every step he tried to take.

Every day, though, it seemed Luke could walk a little better. Before I knew it, he was walking perfectly! The injury did not bother him at all. Because the muscle in that area was damaged, he was 'sween-nied'. When a fly or bug lands on a cow or horse, their skin twitches to remove it. If they are 'sween-nied' in that area, their skin will no longer twitch.

Now that Luke was healed, the fun began!

6

LEARNING

Although a young horse likes to romp and play, there is a lot they need to learn. They need to learn to be around people. They need to learn to lead. They need to learn to be saddled. Most importantly, they need to learn to be ridden.

Before Luke reached the age of two, I prepared him to be ridden. I saddled Luke, or put the saddle on him many times. This helps a horse accept a person on his back, not just a saddle.

When a horse reaches the age of two, they can start learning how to carry a person. This is an exciting stage in their life. It now was time for Luke to become a saddle horse!

At the time Luke was supposed to start being ridden, I was training a horse of my father's. His name was Diamond. He was a beautiful

blood bay. That means he wore an attractive, deep reddish-brown coat. A bay's mane, tail and leg bottoms are always black.

Diamond also carried a star. A star is a white spot found on only the forehead of a horse. His star was in the shape of a diamond. Diamond's name was perfect for him!

White found on a horse's head or legs is called the horse's 'markings'.

Since I was busy riding Diamond, my brother Gary rode Luke the first few times. With the wonderful disposition Luke had, he gave Gary no problems.

A horse must learn to respond to what the rider asks of it. This takes much time riding the horse. During this time, the rider and horse become very attached to one another. They really learn to respond to each other!

Luke and I had many nice rides together. Sometimes, I rode him in a riding arena where I lived. It was oval, in the shape of an egg. The arena was large enough so the horse could move freely when loping. A lope is when the horse is running with a long, easy stride.

The sides of the arena were made of wood which had greyed from the weather. They were a little higher than the back of a horse.

I was riding Luke in the arena one sunny day. White, marshmallow-like clouds gentle crossed the ocean of blue above. It was a peaceful day. You could hear the water rippling across the rocks in the creek. We rode right against

the edge. This was so Luke could learn to turn into the side of the arena. Round and round we went. Both of us were in a lull, enjoying the sun's rays dropping over us. Neither of us noticed my cat, Monty, sitting on top of the fence. He was like a snowball sitting there as he was pure white.

All of a sudden, Luke 'goosed', or jumped forward quickly. I could not imagine what was going on. Looking behind to see what scared him, I was amazed. There, sitting behind the saddle on Luke's rear end, was Monty. He must have thought, "I want to ride around, too."

Luke's reaction to Monty's wanting to ride made Monty quickly dismount, or get off.

Luke was learning to be ridden. Monty learned never to ride a horse again!

Our greatest learning was yet to come!

7

THE SCARE

Luke and I rode for hours on end. Luke learned to accept things he had never seen before. Graceful deer sometimes jumped in front of us. Although Luke and Pete were friends, strange dogs tried to scare him. Spooked birds of all sorts flew from underneath him. Even snakes slithered through his legs to escape the haunting hooves, the horse's feet.

One dismal day we had been riding for a long time. The dark clouds seemed to hang from the sky. With every minute, the day became gloomier.

We had ridden in a circle and were close to home. I knew it would only take a few minutes to get to the house. Thunder started rolling through the sky. I was happy to be so close to home.

Then Luke stopped solid in his tracks. There in front of us was a deep ravine, or ditch. There was no way we could get down it. Large rocks covered the slopes.

The walls of the ravine were almost straight up and down. I did not know what we were going to do.

To go back around would take hours. Now lightning was shooting through the menacing sky. Luke's ears were up with every crack of lightning and roar of thunder. I could not imagine how the sky could become any darker.

Over to the side of us was an old train trestle. That is a bridge for trains. It is not solid. The tracks go straight while underneath them, going crossways, are wide pieces of wood, or crossbeams. In between those 'crossbeams' is a wide, open space. Looking through these open spaces, you see clear down to the bottom of the ravine.

We went and stood by the trestle. I look carefully at each crossbeam. I looked in the direction of the house and back at the trestle. "I wonder if we could make it across this.", I questioned.

If we crossed the trestle, Luke would have to make sure every step landed on the crossbeam. If he missed, his leg would drop through to nothing below. If this happened, his leg could get stuck. Worse yet, if Luke's leg went through, he could get scared, or spook, and break his leg.

The storm kept getting worse. I had to make a decision fast. It was either turn around and ride back for hours or take the chance of crossing the trestle.

Finally I turned Luke around. We started the long trek back home the way we had come. As we left that ominous trestle, the sun started shining through the dark clouds. In an instant, the clouds all disappeared. The deep blue sky was smiling down upon us.

I was very upset realizing I had even considered putting Luke at risk. We eventually made it home. It was a wonderful ride with the sun's rays leading us, the birds singing their songs, flowers greeting us and knowing everything was okay.

 I learned more than Luke that day. I learned never take a chance of putting a horse in harms way. Everything will work out.

Luke then went on to do his work!

8

GATHERING

The most important job a horse
does on a ranch is gather cows.
Once grass in a pasture has been
eaten, the cattle must be moved to
a different pasture. The pasture
used depends on the time of year.
A pasture in the mountains can not
be used in Winter as it is carpeted
with icy, white snow. Pasture near

the house needs to be saved for when the calves are young.

Gary and I were going to help some neighbors move their cattle to a different pasture. Their ranch was in the mountains. Towering mountain peaks looked down upon the ranch. Tall, green pine trees covered the pasture. The cows were going to a pasture near the Big Hole River in Southern Montana.

This was Luke's first, 'big' cattle drive. He had only been ridden a few times.

The day started out to be sunny and bright. In the mountains, though, the weather changes rapid-ly.

There were several riders and every color of horse imaginable. There were black, brown, blue and red horses. Tick was even there. Years later, he belonged to me.

Luke did not know what to think with all these strange horses around. His fluffy ears stood straight up. He did not know which horse to look at.

Once we got around the cows, though, Luke did not care about the other horses. His concern was finding a cow behind each massive pine tree we came upon. Behind every bush, Luke looked for a calf. We had to be careful not to leave behind any calves. If a cow does not know where her baby is, she will want to look for it.

There were hundreds of cows and calves in this pasture. I knew it was going to be difficult getting them all gathered to start pushing them to their new pasture. The pasture was many miles away.

"Hut, hut, hut", riders hollered out.

"Get up there," others screamed.

Once the cows knew they were supposed to be moving, out from behind the trees they came running. It was though every tree hid several cows and calves. Calves tried to keep up, bawling, or crying out, the whole way.

Cows, calves and bulls (the calves fathers) came running in every direction. As they grouped together into a large mass of red and black, calves were separated from their mothers. The cows were extremely nervous not having their babies beside them. I had never seen cows this nervous. Hundreds and hundreds kept running to join together.

Luke kept up with the cattle. He, like the other horses, was unusually nervous. The cows' continual bawling joined together with the crying of the calves to fill the air.

Once all of the cattle were together, we started pushing them. Cows kept looking back, calling for their calves. Calves kept looking ahead, crying for their moms. It was a constant struggle to keep them moving.

The sky was changing and so was our job!

9

THE STORM

The smell of the fresh pine trees had been covered by the smell of cows and horses. A stiff breeze was now filling the air with the smell of storm.

As the breeze turned into a strong wind, the sunny, blue sky filled with treacherous, black clouds. Thunder began pounding through the trees. Lightning started bolting in every direction.

The critters now became terribly nervous. As they moved forward, they danced from side to side. Their cries were engulfed by the roaring thunder. The furious wind pelted us with hard, cold rain. Cows, calves, bulls and horses alike put their heads to the ground to protect them. There was no pro-

tection to be found.

Luke did not know what to think. He had been in storms. There had never been any this severe. He knew he was to watch the cows. The continually "pop, pop, pop" of the lightning and "roar, roar, roar" of the thunder kept him from doing so. If you brought your face up, it was filled with ravaging rain.

Keeping the cows and their babies moving forward was difficult. The riders' hollers to keep them moving were muted by the storm.

A cow turned to look for her calf. The rider behind her pushed her back. Another cow did the same. The rider following her turned her back. Cow after cow kept turning, wanting to find their babies. They wanted to protect them from the raging storm. They did not want to continue facing it.

It took a lot of work on the riders' part to keep turning the cows back. The horses had to run back and forth behind the cows to keep them moving. The riders had to holler continually to order the cows to move ahead.

Every time one cow turned back, another did. When two turned back, four did. Then......it happened. All of them turned back. Cows, calves and bulls were turned, facing us.

As soon as the herd turned, there was a tremendous, "CRRRACK". Lightning struck right above our heads. A blinding flash surrounded us.

Immediately the herd started running. Right at us they swarmed. We all hollered as we ran our horses back and forth to block the herd. Luke was scared, but he kept working. Back and forth he ran. Nothing stopped the herd. They did not even slow down.

Luke did not know what to do when cows ran past both sides of him. Calves zipped by frantically. Massive bulls thundered past, not slowing at all by the horses.

The herd of hundreds was finally gone. Through the solid sheet of rain, they were barely seen. There was nothing to be done to stop them. They did not ease up until they got back to their original pasture. There, the cows located their babies and huddled together.

Through it all, Luke did his best. Although it was his first cattle drive, it would not be his last.

There was more to Luke, though, then just a saddle horse!

10

THE BOND

Luke and I went on many cattle drives and rides together. All of them were a joy. They are memories that can never be replaced.

An individual and a horse, when working together, form a bond, or close friendship, like no other. When a person raises and trains a horse, this bond is even stronger. You learn together. You grow together. You age together. You also share together.

No relationship is the same with every horse. Each horse has a different personality. Each relationship is different with every horse. Each relationship is one you will relish forever.

Luke was a good friend I enjoyed sharing my life with. I will always remember and cherish him.

ZC HORSES SERIES

Now that you have met Luke, you can read about Chick's next baby, Barbie! Read the about joy of breaking, training, working with and riding her. Get to know her better and hear her story. You will fall in love with this horse after reading the fifth in the **'ZC HORSES'** series, *"BARBIE-THE BEST"*.
Be sure to be there to greet her!!

ZC HORSES SERIES #5

Barbie - The Best!

by Diane W. Keaster

Coming October 2002

To My Reader:

I was born and raised on a ranch near a little town called Belt, Montana. After receiving my B.S. in Business Education from Montana State University, I taught high school business. I then moved on to other facets of employment.

The whole time, I was team roping and raising, breaking and training horses. The profession I fell into by mistake was trading horses. Throughout my life, I have handled hundreds of horses, all which have a story of their own.

I have two sons, Cole and Augustus, who also rope and have a love for and talent with horses. We ride our horses for enjoyment into mountain lakes, help local ranchers with their cattle, golf, water ski, downhill ski and snowboard, cross-country ski, fish, roller blade, ride bike and laugh together. We have dogs, cats, rabbits, chickens, ducks, geese, fish, and George, the parrot. We live near the beautiful Salmon River at Salmon, Idaho.

My boys loved reading stories about horses and I loved reading the stories to them. That is why I am writing these books. I want to tell the stories of the creatures I love to the children I love.

I thank Jehovah our Creator for giving us such a wonderful, beautiful animal!

What about Chick? She is still enjoying her retirement on my mother's ranch at Belt, visiting with my mom's and brother Gary's horses.

Enjoy the stories!

Order Form
ZC HORSES SERIES

Don't miss out on any part of the lives of Chick and her many babies and friends! Experience all of the rides, joys and sorrows. Don't be left out!

___ Chick-The Beginning! (Spring 2001)	$6.95
___ Chick-The Saddle Horse! (Summer 2001)	$6.95
___ Chick-The Mom! (March 2002)	$6.95
___ Luke-The First! (July 2002)	$6.95
___ Barbie-The Best! (Oct. 2002)	$6.95
___ZC Leather-tooled Bookmarks	$3.00

UPCOMING TITLES

Chickadee-The Traveler!	Goldie-The Smart!
Tawny-The Beauty!	Sonny-The Spectacular!
Onie-The Roanie!	Belle-The Sweetie!
Classy-The Special!	Lily-The Pretty Paint!
Black Jack-The Great !	Leroy-The Prize!
Slick-The Friend!	Apple-The Joy!

Also read about Cider, Buck, Nellie, Junie, Eagle, Smokey, Sarge, Tex, Radar and many more!

ZC HORSES SERIES, 701 S. St. Chas., Salmon, ID 83467
(208) 756-3757
geocities.com/zchorses Email: zchorses@hotmail.com
Please send me the books I have checked above. I am enclosing US $____(please add $2/bk to cover shipping and handling). Send check or money order, please.

NAME_____

ADDRESS_____

CITY/STATE/ZIP_____

PHONE(OPTIONAL)_____
Please allow four to six weeks for delivery. Shipping prices good in U.S. only. Prices subject to change.